The USPTO Patent Bar Exam

Ultimate Study Guide, Test Prep, and Exam Strategy Overview

By Wysebridge.com

February 2024

www.wysebridge.com

Introduction

Welcome aspiring patent practitioner. Whether you are familiar with patent law and intellectual property matters, you are in the right place.

The Journey Begins

In the early days of 2011 and 2012, a few of us found ourselves grappling with the challenges of preparing for the patent bar exam. Our frustrations were manifold:

- The prohibitive costs associated with every study program available.
- A notable lack of personalized support.
- Difficulties in finding reliable guidance.
- The outdated nature of study materials (think shipping CDs).

These hurdles led us to meticulously analyze the patent bar exam. It became clear that existing preparation programs were falling short. Many were either overly simplistic, glossing over the exam's complexities, or overly detailed, aiming to make candidates patent law experts—a far cry from the exam's actual requirements. Even more disheartening was the steep financial burden these programs imposed.

Wysebridge.com Patent Bar Review: The Genesis

We came to understand the exam for what it truly was: a barrier to entry. Simply put, answer enough questions correctly, and you pass. This realization was our turning point. It wasn't about measuring your depth of knowledge but about navigating a multiple-choice test effectively.

Armed with this insight, we embarked on applying proven learning strategies, tailoring our study materials to what we needed. It wasn't long before we recognized the formula for success: a blend of knowledge and skill, coupled with confidence and a supportive network to persevere through inevitable frustrations.

We started tutoring and sharing our evolving materials with peers. The success rates soared, and it became evident—we had crafted a winning approach. Our team, passionate about aiding others, was committed to offering this resource widely and affordably.

The Birth of Wysebridge

Wysebridge emerged from a genuine desire to assist—not just ourselves but also our peers—in navigating the patent bar exam with less stress and greater efficiency. Merging our post-AIA insights with expertise from IP professionals and chief legal officers, and fueled by a love for data and analysis, we created an entirely online community. This community caters to the new wave of exam candidates, providing a comprehensive, accessible, and community-driven approach to conquering the patent bar exam.

Transitioning to Patent Law? Start Here

Navigating the World of Patent Law: A Primer for Beginners

If you're stepping into the realm of patent law for the first time, this section is crafted just for you. The landscape of patent law, its processes, and the patent bar exam might initially seem daunting. Yet, when you dive deeper, you'll find that patent law, by comparison to other legal areas, maintains a level of consistency that facilitates learning, especially when the information is presented effectively.

Your Go-To Resource: The MPEP

At the heart of patent law learning and practice is the Manual of Patent Examining Procedure, widely known as the MPEP. This comprehensive guide is indispensable for both patent examiners and those aspiring to become patent agents or attorneys. It includes everything essential for preparing and prosecuting patents, with appendices that detail the law itself. While a printed copy might not be readily available for purchase as a single volume, securing a printed version for your study and reference is crucial. It becomes, in essence, your patent law bible.

Exam Preparation: Mastering the MPEP

During the patent bar exam, you'll have access to a complete electronic version of the MPEP, laws included, via a PDF reader on your exam computer. It's vital to not only possess your own copy for preparation but also to become proficient in navigating this document to quickly find answers and relevant material.

International Context: The PCT

For international patent applications, the guiding framework is the Patent Cooperation Treaty (PCT), which outlines how its 150+ signatory countries must examine and recognize patents, provided those applications comply with the treaty's procedures. The PCT rules, found in Appendices P and T of the MPEP, are a critical study area for the USPTO Patent Bar Exam.

The Essence of Patent Law

Patent law is concise. Prior to the America Invents Act (AIA), it occupied just 88 pages within the voluminous MPEP, located in Appendix L for Law. The AIA introduced 37 new sections, expanding the legal landscape. This brevity and structure of patent law make it a unique and fascinating field of study, challenging future practitioners to grasp its nuances and apply them adeptly.

Understanding the Hierarchy of Patent Law Resources

Following the foundational layers of law and treaties, we delve into the realm of Regulations, crafted by the United States Patent and Trademark Office (USPTO). These Regulations, also known as Rules (conveniently both starting with "R" and found in Appendix R), form a critical component of patent law governance. Published as Title 37 of the Code of Federal Regulations, abbreviated as 37 CFR, these sections sometimes feature the section symbol (§).

Court Cases: The Role of Judicial Precedents

Another pivotal source of patent law is the jurisprudence of the Federal Circuit and appellate courts. Since its inception in 1982, the United States Court of Appeals for the Federal Circuit (CAFC) has significantly shaped patent law. While the exam won't require in-depth knowledge of court decisions, many current patent practices are named after landmark cases. Although CAFC decisions technically supersede USPTO Regulations, conflicts in practice are rare and need not concern you at this stage. Court cases become more relevant as you embark on actual patent practice.

The MPEP: A Comprehensive Guide

Beyond Regulations and court cases lie the Procedures detailed in the MPEP, guiding both patent examiners and candidates through the intricate steps of patent processing. The MPEP is structured into 29 chapters and 7 appendices, logically arranged to cover the journey from filing to patent grant, including post-grant corrections.

A crucial task for candidates is to memorize key chapter numbers and topics. For efficient exam navigation, it's best to search by topic or chapter, as the MPEP's index can be overwhelming in its complexity.

When encountering references like "Chapter 2100," it indicates a specific section within the MPEP. For example, 2133.03(c) refers to section 2133 in chapter 2100, highlighting the structured and accessible nature of this reference material.

Despite its formidable size and occasional complexities, the MPEP is surprisingly user-friendly, offering examples to facilitate learning.

Keeping Up-to-Date with the MPEP

The MPEP is regularly updated by the USPTO to reflect legal changes and court rulings. These updates ensure that the material remains relevant and accurate for both exam preparation and practical patent examination.

Recap: The Study Hierarchy

As you prepare for the patent bar exam, keep this hierarchy in mind for efficient study and reference:
- Law: United States Code Title 35, e.g., 35 USC 102(a) (MPEP Appendix L)
- Law: Patent Cooperation Treaty (PCT) (MPEP Appendices P and T)

- Regulations: Title 37 of the Code of Federal Regulations, e.g., 37 CFR 1.495(b) (MPEP Appendix R)
- Court Cases: Federal Circuit (CAFC) decisions, occasionally Supreme Court rulings
- MPEP Chapters: e.g., §2133.03(c)

Updates to the MPEP and relevant exam materials are provided to ensure that candidates have access to the most current information, with ongoing support for students through email updates following registration.

Mastering the Material: A Guide to Our Program

While no resource is flawless, including the wysebridge.com program, it has been meticulously crafted to align as close as possible with the content of the USPTO's test material resources. Below is an overview of some of the resources available through the Wysebridge.com Patent Bar Review program.

Targeted Study Modules

Wysebridge.com Patent Bar Review has meticulously developed Targeted Study Modules, designed with a strategic approach to enhance your preparation for the Patent Bar Exam. Recognizing the vast array of topics covered in the exam, we've honed in on the areas most frequently tested, allowing you to allocate your study time more efficiently and effectively. This focus on high-yield topics enables candidates to study smarter, not harder, optimizing both preparation time and scoring potential.

Key Features of Targeted Study Modules:

- High-Yield Topics: Each module concentrates on specific areas of patent law that have historically been emphasized on the exam. By understanding these key topics, you're better positioned to tackle the questions most likely to appear.
- Streamlined Learning: The modules distill complex legal principles into digestible, manageable sections, making it easier to grasp challenging concepts and retain crucial information.
- Strategic Question Analysis: Beyond content review, the modules include analysis of question formats and strategies for approaching different types of questions, equipping you with the tools to navigate tricky exam scenarios confidently.
- Practice Questions: Embedded within each module are practice questions mirroring the style and substance of the actual exam. This hands-on approach reinforces learning and improves problem-solving speed and accuracy.
- Adaptive Learning Paths: Recognizing that each candidate's background and learning style are unique, Wysebridge's modules offer adaptive learning paths. This flexibility allows you to focus on strengthening areas of weakness while reinforcing your existing knowledge base.
- Comprehensive Resources: Each module is supplemented with detailed references to the Manual of Patent Examining Procedure (MPEP), enabling candidates to explore topics in depth and understand the legal basis behind exam questions.
- Progress Tracking: Integrated tools allow you to monitor your advancement through the modules, providing insight into your readiness and areas needing further review.

Benefits of Targeted Study Modules:

- Efficiency: By concentrating your efforts on the most tested topics, you reduce study time while increasing the effectiveness of your preparation.
- Confidence: Familiarity with high-yield topics builds confidence, reducing exam-day stress and improving overall performance.
- Depth of Understanding: Deep dives into complex subjects ensure a robust comprehension of patent law's nuances, preparing you for both the exam and future practice.
- Flexibility: The modular structure caters to diverse learning preferences and schedules, making it easier to fit exam preparation into busy lives.
- Community Support: Access to Wysebridge's community provides additional motivation and support, connecting you with peers and experts for advice and encouragement.

Through the Targeted Study Modules, Wysebridge Patent Bar Review empowers you to approach the Patent Bar Exam with confidence, armed with knowledge and strategies tailored to the exam's most critical aspects.

Exam Simulator & Practice Question Module

Wysebridge Patent Bar Review's platform elevates your exam preparation with Your Own Exam Simulator, a dynamic tool designed to closely replicate the experience of taking the actual Patent Bar Exam. This innovative feature not only simulates the exam environment but also integrates instant feedback and comprehensive analytics, enabling you to refine your test-taking strategies, address your weaknesses, and build confidence as your exam date approaches.

Core Components of Your Own Exam Simulator:

- Realistic Exam Conditions: The simulator is crafted to provide a way to practice questions in a format similar to the actual exam. That said, we did not create an exact replica. Why? Because the prometric software on the day of the exam is (to be blunt) quite annoying. It is a far better use of your time and energy to simply look at the prometric demo of the platform and exam software and familiarize with the feel that way, and then practice on a system that allows for a better user experience (and ease of review, etc) and is a faster platform overall.
- Instant Feedback: Immediately after answering questions, you'll receive feedback, including detailed explanations and references to the relevant sections of the Manual of Patent Examining Procedure (MPEP). This instant feedback is crucial for understanding mistakes and learning the correct concepts on the spot. You also have the option to practice without this feature (Which then mimics the real exam).
- Analytics and Performance Tracking: The simulator tracks your performance across various topics, offering insights into your strengths and areas for improvement. These

analytics help you to tailor your study focus, ensuring you spend time on the topics that will most impact your exam score.

- Topical Quiz Practice: Beyond full-length practice exams, the simulator offers quizzes focused on specific topics, allowing for targeted practice. Whether you're struggling with patentability requirements, USPTO procedures, or any other area, these quizzes help reinforce your understanding of key concepts.
- Repeating Missed Answers: A unique feature of the simulator is its ability to present questions you've previously missed, enabling focused review and reinforcement of those topics. This iterative learning process ensures that you not only recognize your mistakes but also solidify your grasp of the correct answers.
- Simulated Exam Mode: Engage in practice exams under timed conditions to improve your time management skills and endurance for the actual exam. Simulated exam mode helps you to develop a strategy for navigating the exam efficiently, ensuring you can complete all questions within the allotted time.

Benefits of Your Own Exam Simulator:

- Enhanced Test-Taking Skills: Regular practice with the simulator helps hone your ability to understand and answer questions accurately under exam conditions, reducing anxiety and improving performance.
- Focused Study Approach: By identifying specific areas of weakness, you can concentrate your study efforts where they are most needed, making your preparation more effective.
- Confidence Building: Familiarity with the exam format and types of questions reduces surprises on exam day, boosting your confidence and readiness.
- Efficient Learning: The feedback loop created by immediate answers, explanations, and the repetition of missed questions accelerates your learning process, enabling you to cover more material in less time.

Your Own Exam Simulator is more than just a practice tool; it's an integral part of your comprehensive study plan with Wysebridge Patent Bar Review, designed to ensure you approach the Patent Bar Exam with confidence, knowledge, and a strategic advantage

Flashcards

Wysebridge Patent Bar Review has meticulously developed an extensive collection of over 1,000 flashcards, tailored to facilitate quick and efficient learning for the Patent Bar Exam. These flashcards are a cornerstone of the study materials provided on wysebridge.com, designed with the candidate's success in mind. Here's an in-depth look at how these flashcards can transform your exam preparation:

Comprehensive Coverage

- Broad Spectrum of Topics: The flashcards cover a wide range of subjects pertinent to the Patent Bar Exam, from the intricacies of patent law to the specific procedures of the USPTO. This comprehensive approach ensures that candidates are well-prepared for any question the exam may present.
- Critical Concepts and Terminology: Each card focuses on essential concepts, legal standards, and terminology that are crucial for understanding patent law and successfully navigating the exam. This targeted approach aids in building a solid foundation of knowledge.

Efficient Learning and Retention

- Quick Assimilation: The concise format of flashcards makes them an ideal tool for rapidly absorbing and internalizing key facts. This efficiency is crucial for candidates balancing exam preparation with other professional and personal commitments.
- Active Recall Practice: Engaging with flashcards encourages active recall, a proven method for enhancing memory retention. This practice strengthens your ability to retrieve information quickly, a critical skill for the timed environment of the Patent Bar Exam.

Flexible and Accessible Study Tool

- Study Anytime, Anywhere: The digital format of the flashcards on wysebridge.com allows for convenient access from any device, enabling you to utilize every spare moment for study, whether you're commuting, on a break, or winding down for the evening.

Engaging and Interactive Learning

- Variety in Presentation: The flashcards employ various methods of presenting information, including question-and-answer formats, diagrams, and bullet points. This variety helps to keep study sessions engaging and prevents the monotony often associated with exam preparation.
- Instant Feedback: Immediate reinforcement of correct answers or clarification of misunderstandings facilitates a dynamic learning experience, allowing for quick adjustments and improved understanding with each session.

Continual Review and Reinforcement

- Cyclical Review System: The design of the flashcard system encourages continual review of material, ensuring that previously studied concepts are revisited and reinforced over time. This cyclical review process is key to long-term retention of information.

- Highlighting Key Information: Important laws, exceptions, and USPTO procedures are emphasized across the flashcards, ensuring that candidates recognize and remember the information most likely to appear on the exam.

The flashcards offered by Wysebridge Patent Bar Review represent a powerful tool in your arsenal for conquering the Patent Bar Exam. By integrating these flashcards into your study plan, you can elevate your preparation, ensuring a comprehensive and deep understanding of the material, readying you for success on exam day and beyond.

Frequency Charts

Wysebridge Patent Bar Review enhances your exam preparation with meticulously crafted Frequency Charts, a strategic tool designed to streamline your study process. By conducting a thorough analysis of past exams and gathering anecdotal evidence from a wide array of sources, these charts pinpoint the topics and concepts that are most frequently tested on the Patent Bar Exam. Here's a closer look at how the Frequency Charts can optimize your study approach:

Data-Driven Insights

- Empirical Analysis: The foundation of the Frequency Charts lies in a rigorous examination of historical exam patterns. This empirical approach ensures that our recommendations are grounded in actual test data, providing you with a reliable guide to the exam's content focus.
- Anecdotal Corroboration: Beyond raw data, anecdotal evidence from past exam takers, including feedback on unexpected questions or recurring themes, is incorporated. This holistic view captures nuances that pure data analysis might overlook, offering a comprehensive picture of potential exam content.

Strategic Study Focus

- Prioritized Topics: With the vast amount of information covered by the Patent Bar Exam, knowing where to focus your efforts can be overwhelming. The Frequency Charts simplify this decision-making process by highlighting the subjects that yield the highest return on investment in terms of study time versus potential exam impact.
- Efficient Preparation: By concentrating on areas with the highest frequency of testing, you can allocate your study time more efficiently, ensuring that you cover the most critical topics thoroughly without getting bogged down in less relevant details.

Enhanced Understanding and Retention

- Targeted Learning: Focusing on high-frequency topics allows for deeper engagement and understanding of core patent law principles and USPTO procedures. This targeted learning approach fosters a stronger grasp of the material, enhancing your ability to apply knowledge effectively under exam conditions.

- Reinforcement of Key Concepts: The charts serve as a continual reference point throughout your study process, reinforcing the importance of certain topics and encouraging repeated review. This reinforcement aids in long-term retention of critical information.

Customizable Study Plans

- Adaptable Strategies: Recognizing that each candidate has unique strengths and weaknesses, the Frequency Charts enable personalized study plans. You can adjust your focus based on your comfort level with various topics, ensuring a customized preparation experience that addresses your specific needs.
- Dynamic Updates: As the USPTO updates exam content and new trends emerge, Wysebridge continually revises the Frequency Charts. This dynamic updating process ensures that you're always studying the most current and relevant material, keeping pace with the evolving landscape of the Patent Bar Exam.

Supportive Study Aid

- Complementary Tool: The Frequency Charts are designed to complement other Wysebridge study materials, including targeted study modules, flashcards, and practice exams. Together, these resources provide a cohesive and comprehensive preparation strategy, grounded in the realities of the Patent Bar Exam.
- Confidence Building: Knowing that your study efforts are concentrated on the most impactful topics can significantly boost your confidence as you approach exam day. This confidence, rooted in thorough and focused preparation, is key to a calm and successful exam experience.
-

Wysebridge Patent Bar Review's Frequency Charts represent a cornerstone of effective exam preparation, guiding you through the vast landscape of patent law with clarity and precision. By integrating these charts into your study regimen, you're not just studying harder—you're studying smarter, with a clear focus on what matters most for exam success.

Detailed MPEP Chapter Summaries and Reviews

Wysebridge Patent Bar Review offers Detailed Chapter Reviews, a crucial resource designed to streamline your understanding of the Manual of Patent Examining Procedure (MPEP). These targeted and detailed summaries distill each chapter of the MPEP, focusing on the most significant aspects that impact your exam performance and practical patent prosecution work. Here's an expanded look at the benefits and features of these reviews:

Deep Dive into MPEP Architecture

- Structured Overview: The Detailed Chapter Reviews provide a structured overview of the MPEP's architecture, allowing candidates to quickly grasp the layout and organization of this extensive resource. Understanding the MPEP's structure is key to efficiently navigating the manual during the exam and in practice.
- Essential Content Focus: By concentrating on the elements that truly matter for the Patent Bar Exam, these reviews eliminate the noise of less relevant information. This focus ensures that your study time is spent on material with the highest likelihood of appearing on the exam.

Enhanced Learning and Retention

- Clear Summaries: Each chapter review is crafted to present clear, concise summaries of complex legal concepts and USPTO procedures. This clarity aids in the rapid assimilation and retention of critical information, making these summaries an invaluable study aid.
- Key Concepts Highlighted: Important laws, rules, and procedures are highlighted within the reviews, drawing attention to the core principles that underpin patent law and the USPTO's operations. This emphasis helps to solidify your understanding of fundamental patent concepts.

Efficient Study Tool

- Time-Saving: The Detailed Chapter Reviews save you time by providing a shortcut to mastering the MPEP, eliminating the need to sift through each chapter in its entirety. This efficiency is crucial for candidates juggling exam preparation with other professional and personal responsibilities.
- Targeted Study Sessions: With the ability to focus on specific chapters or topics, you can tailor your study sessions to address areas where you need the most review. This targeted approach maximizes the effectiveness of your study time.

Practical Application

- Real-World Relevance: Beyond exam preparation, the understanding of the MPEP gained through these chapter reviews is directly applicable to your future work in patent law. The practical insights offered by these summaries will serve you well in patent prosecution and beyond.
- Strategic Insights: The reviews also offer strategic insights into navigating the patent examination process, providing candidates with a deeper understanding of how to approach patent applications effectively.

Complementary Study Resource

- Integration with Other Materials: The Detailed Chapter Reviews are designed to work hand in hand with Wysebridge's other study materials, including frequency charts, flashcards, and practice exams. Together, these resources offer a comprehensive preparation strategy that covers all angles of the exam.
- Dynamic Updates: As the MPEP is updated and exam trends evolve, Wysebridge ensures that the chapter reviews are revised accordingly. This commitment to currency means you're always studying the most up-to-date information available.

Wysebridge Patent Bar Review's Detailed Chapter Reviews are more than just summaries—they are a strategic tool designed to enhance your understanding of the MPEP, streamline your study process, and prepare you for success on the Patent Bar Exam and in your future patent practice.

Detailed AIA Summaries and Reviews

Wysebridge Patent Bar Review's AIA & Rules Summary is an indispensable resource for candidates preparing for the Patent Bar Exam, especially in light of the significant changes introduced by the America Invents Act (AIA). This comprehensive summary is meticulously designed to help you take control of your exam preparation by mastering the latest updates and understanding how they affect the Manual of Patent Examining Procedure (MPEP). Here's an expanded overview of what this crucial study aid offers:

Comprehensive Coverage of AIA Updates

- Thorough Analysis: The AIA & Rules Summary offers a thorough analysis of the post-AIA changes, ensuring that you have a deep understanding of how these updates have transformed patent law and practice. This analysis is crucial for anyone aiming to excel on the Patent Bar Exam and in their future work as a patent practitioner.
- Clear Explanations: Complex legal changes are broken down into clear, manageable explanations. This approach makes it easier to grasp the nuances of the AIA and how it impacts various aspects of patent law, from filing procedures to patentability criteria.

Detailed Reviews of MPEP Changes

- Section-by-Section Insights: Our summaries provide detailed insights into each relevant section of the MPEP that has been affected by the AIA. This section-by-section review ensures that you're aware of the most current rules and procedures as outlined by the USPTO.
- Focus on What Matters: By highlighting the most significant changes and how they apply to exam questions and real-world patent prosecution, the AIA & Rules Summary helps you focus your study on what really matters, maximizing your preparation efficiency.

Strategic Study Aid

- Targeted Learning: The summary is designed to target your learning towards the most impactful AIA updates. This targeted approach helps you efficiently master the material that is most likely to appear on the exam, ensuring a strategic and focused study regimen.
- Integration with Practice Questions: To reinforce your understanding of the AIA updates, the summary is integrated with practice questions that reflect these changes. This hands-on approach solidifies your knowledge and prepares you for the types of questions you'll encounter on the exam.

Up-to-Date Information

- Regular Updates: The AIA & Rules Summary is regularly updated to reflect any further changes to the MPEP or additional clarifications provided by the USPTO. This commitment to providing the most current information ensures that you're always studying the most relevant material.

Confidence Building

- Boost Your Confidence: By mastering the AIA updates with our comprehensive summaries, you'll approach the Patent Bar Exam with increased confidence, knowing that you're fully prepared to tackle questions on the most recent aspects of patent law.

Practical Benefits Beyond the Exam

- Real-World Application: Understanding the AIA and its implications is not only essential for passing the Patent Bar Exam but also for your future career in patent law. Our AIA & Rules Summary equips you with knowledge that will be directly applicable in your practice, enhancing your capabilities as a patent professional.

Wysebridge Patent Bar Review's AIA & Rules Summary is more than just a study aid; it's a strategic tool designed to ensure that you're fully versed in the latest developments in patent law, giving you the knowledge and confidence to excel on the Patent Bar Exam and in your subsequent patent practice.

Test Taking Strategies

The Patent Bar Exam unfolds over a single day, divided into two three-hour sessions, one in the morning and the other in the afternoon, each comprising 50 multiple-choice questions (options A through E). While you can review and revise your answers within each session, the morning and afternoon sessions operate independently of each other.

The Importance of a Solid Test Strategy

The margin between passing and failing this exam is often narrow, with many candidates missing the mark by just a handful of questions. The exam is designed to challenge you at every turn; there are no real freebee questions here. The only caveat is that you may encounter some repeat questions from prior exams. While this is FAR less common than it once was, it still happens. Thus, spending time using Wysebridge.com's frequently asked questions and frequency charts can provide you with an immediate leg up on the exam.

Finishing the exam is a hurdle for many. Mastery of the material and the ability to maintain focus and speed for extended periods are crucial. Ideally, you'll manage your time such that you have a few minutes at the end of each session to review your answers or research the ones you're unsure about. Based on our experience, allocating 2-5 minutes per question for review and lookup is realistic, allowing you to revisit three or four questions at most in each session.

Key takeaways for effective preparation and strategy include:
- In-depth Knowledge: Aim to have a firm understanding on at least 90% of the material. Prioritize understanding the concepts highlighted in the study materials that we've highlighted as the most crucial to know.
- Confidence Marking System: Develop a method for noting how confident you feel about each answer. This will enable you to utilize any remaining time at the end of each session efficiently.
- Efficient Lookup Skills: Being adept at quickly finding information within the provided materials can be a significant advantage.

Expect all questions to challenge your understanding and application of patent law.

Implementing Your Test Strategy

I recommend adopting a systematic approach to tracking your confidence in your answers, which will directly inform your review and lookup strategy during the exam. We suggest using the concept of an "answer grid", followed by guidance on leveraging this grid for an effective review process.

Please refer to Fig. 1 below for an example of how to set up your answer grid.

Figure 1: Wysebridge.com Answer Sheet Template

COMMENTS   COMMENTS

1 A   B   C   D   E   26 A   B   C   D   E
2 A   B   C   D   E   27 A   B   C   D   E
3 A   B   C   D   E   28 A   B   C   D   E
4 A   B   C   D   E   29 A   B   C   D   E
5 A   B   C   D   E   30 A   B   C   D   E
6 A   B   C   D   E   31 A   B   C   D   E
7 A   B   C   D   E   32 A   B   C   D   E
8 A   B   C   D   E   33 A   B   C   D   E
9 A   B   C   D   E   34 A   B   C   D   E
10 A   B   C   D   E   35 A   B   C   D   E
11 A   B   C   D   E   36 A   B   C   D   E
12 A   B   C   D   E   37 A   B   C   D   E
13 A   B   C   D   E   38 A   B   C   D   E
14 A   B   C   D   E   39 A   B   C   D   E
15 A   B   C   D   E   40 A   B   C   D   E
16 A   B   C   D   E   41 A   B   C   D   E
17 A   B   C   D   E   42 A   B   C   D   E
18 A   B   C   D   E   43 A   B   C   D   E
19 A   B   C   D   E   44 A   B   C   D   E
20 A   B   C   D   E   45 A   B   C   D   E
21 A   B   C   D   E   46 A   B   C   D   E
22 A   B   C   D   E   47 A   B   C   D   E
23 A   B   C   D   E   48 A   B   C   D   E
24 A   B   C   D   E   49 A   B   C   D   E
25 A   B   C   D   E   50 A   B   C   D   E

So, here's your strategic approach for the exam day. Upon entering the testing room, you'll be provided with scratch paper and pencils. Your first move? Construct your answer sheet template. You might wonder why this step is crucial. Consider this perspective: setting a pre-exam goal like creating an answer sheet template, and achieving it as soon as you're seated at the computer, serves as an initial win. Entering the exam room, it's natural for your nerves to be heightened and your heart to be racing. Completing a task you planned boosts your confidence and calms your nerves. It offers a tangible proof of your capability right at the outset—"I've already accomplished one of my goals for today." This achievement sets a positive tone, allowing you to start the exam feeling organized and focused.

Contrast this approach with diving straight into the exam and being greeted by a potentially challenging first question. This scenario can feel like a metaphorical "slap in the face," overwhelming you and potentially triggering panic. However, having the answer template ready acts as a psychological safety net, reminding you, "I've got this. I successfully created my answer template. Time to move forward." This methodical preparation not only prepares you logistically for the exam but also puts you in the right mental space to tackle the questions with confidence and clarity.

Before the clock starts ticking on your Patent Bar Exam, you're granted up to fifteen minutes with the testing computer. This period is intended for familiarizing yourself with the exam interface through instructional screens. These instructions are accessible beforehand on the USPTO website, so it's advisable to review them prior to your exam date to free up these precious minutes for setting up your answer sheet template for strategic use during the test.

Given that you'll tackle 50 questions per session, organize the first page of your scratch paper into columns as above. Leave a blank colum space on the left of your page. An inch maybe. Then the first column write out the question number 1-25 or 1-50, depending on how you setup your paper, and then mark the letters A, B, C, D, and E on the right side of each number. Then, leave a space to the right for comments/notes you might make during the exam.

This layout serves as your answer grid for the session's questions. Remember, you'll need to create a new grid for the afternoon session, as you'll exchange your used scratch paper for fresh sheets.

For each question option, employ one of three indicators: a Circle around the letter for correct answers, a line/dash through the letter for known incorrect ones, and either a question mark or no mark for "unsure" answers. Furthermore, circle the question number itself once you've satisfied to yourself that the question is "done" (meaning, you don't need to review it and that is your final answer that you've marked on the sheet).

This method, illustrated in Fig. 2, is essential for an efficient review process and is preferable to using the exam software's "Mark" feature. Why? Because the software is notoriously difficult to work with, and is NOT as effective as the method above. Additionally, there is no way to keep track of notes or when you know an answer is wrong.

Figure 2: Example of Wysebridge.com Answer Sheet Template in use

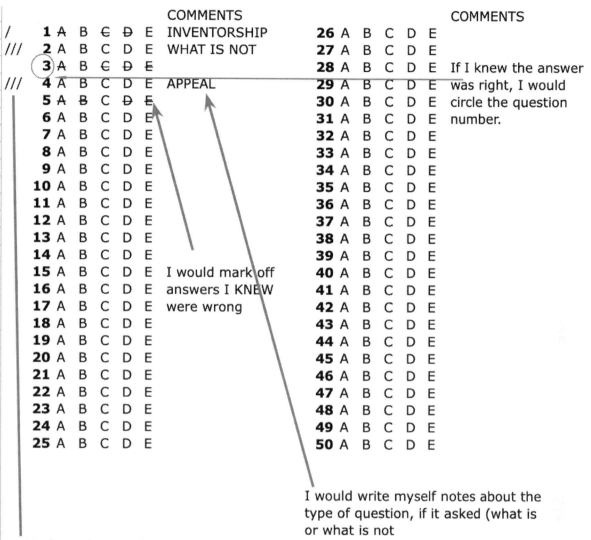

With this methodology, you'll end up with a clear pattern of elimination for each question, aiming for one circled letter and four crossed out letters for most questions, as seen in Fig. 2.

When faced with questions framed negatively (asking which answer is not correct), maintain the same marking system to avoid confusion. We encourage you to actually write the word "except" or "no" down on the sheet as well. This consistency helps in managing double negatives and ensuring you don't overlook the word "not" in the question's phrasing.

Always read all five answer choices thoroughly. It's common to identify two seemingly correct answers on the first pass, necessitating a closer comparison to discern the best choice or to catch any initial oversights.

If guessing becomes necessary, retain your original markings on the scratch paper. These indicators will guide you during any possible review periods, allowing you to quickly revisit your strongest contenders for a more in-depth evaluation or lookup.

Your strategy for tackling the exam should start with a preliminary review of all 50 questions, allocating roughly an hour for this phase. During this initial walkthrough, eliminate any answers you're certain are incorrect, jot down any pertinent thoughts next to the question, and then proceed to the next one. For questions where you're confident in the answer, mark the question number with a circle to signify that you've found the correct response. For items where you're completely unsure, denote your uncertainty with three hash marks.

After reviewing all questions in this manner, revisit each one systematically, utilizing the MPEP index to verify the correct answers. Once you've confidently identified an answer in the MPEP, note it on your answer sheet and in the exam software, then encircle the question number. This circle symbolizes completion. Additionally, marking the correct answer on your sheet provides a quick reference to double-check your selections against the computer program before final submission. This method helped me spot two instances where I had mistakenly selected the wrong answer in the exam software, allowing me to correct these errors before completing the exam.

Here's a concise guide on how to effectively utilize your answer grid during the exam:

Answer Confidence Marking Explained

- **High Confidence:** If you're highly certain of an answer (and or conversely, highly confident of a wrong answer) - cross out the incorrect answers and circle the correct. Place a single hash to the left of the question number.
- **Moderate Confidence:** If you feel confident but wish to double-check later, put one or two hashes next to the question number
- **Uncertain but Know Where to Look:** Place one or two hashes next to the question number and write down that MPEP section or reference in the comments.
- **No Clue:** If you're at a loss for the answer, put three hashes next to the question number.

Efficient Exam Strategy

Avoid dwelling too long on any single question. If an answer seems reachable but time-consuming, categorize it as a 1 or 2 hash and proceed with your best guess for the moment. However, ensure you briefly review each question right after answering, spending about 20 seconds to internally justify your choice. This quick verification helps catch and correct simple mistakes, like misreading the question or overlooking a critical detail.

Structured Review Process

After reviewing all questions, commence your review by bypassing those you've marked with high confidence and or known answer (these would be circled question numbers).

Reassess the questions marked with a single dash next, deciding whether to confirm your initial answer, or start the process of eliminating the wrong answers/finding the right answer. Once completed, circle the correct answer and question number, and move on.

Next, tackle the double hashes questions. Jot down the specific MPEP section to consult for each of these questions. Aim to spend no more than 2-4 minutes per lookup. If the answer eludes you, make an educated guess and move on.

Finally, circle to the questions with three hashes (the hardest). These often pertain to obscure details designed to test your research skills. Identify unique phrases within the question or answers and use them to pinpoint the relevant section in the MPEP. This strategy can lead you directly to the information needed to resolve these tricky questions.

This should leave you with 3-5 minutes to ensure that all the answers you have done a LOT of hard work ensuring that are now on your answer sheet template, are indeed the answers you've selected on the exam software. Ensure they match. Seriously-make sure what you've circled on your paper is indeed what is selected on the software.

The "phrase search" method can be particularly effective for tackling questions you've marked with 2 or three hashes. As you review each question, keep an eye out for any sequence of two to five words that stands out as being uniquely specific to the topic at hand. If you stumble upon such a phrase, opting for a text search in the MPEP's PDF files could prove more efficient than navigating through topics manually. Common terms like "abandoned" or "obvious," however, are unlikely to yield useful results due to their frequent occurrence across various contexts.

If an answer eludes you, making an educated guess is your next best move. Before guessing:
- Eliminate with Caution: Methodically assess each option, aiming to discard it only if you're confident it's incorrect. This elimination process requires a mindset shift from seeking the right answer to identifying definitively wrong choices.
- Apply Common Sense: Question what seems logical or consistent within the context of patent procedures, which are generally designed for uniformity and fairness. For example, consider the implausibility of arbitrary limits on reference citations by examiners or the relevance of sales data as a standalone proof of non-obviousness.

The MPEP, accessible as searchable PDF files during the exam, is split into chapters and appendices.

Effective Searching Tips:

- Aim to search for distinctive phrases over individual words for more precise results. The answers provided in the questions often contain the exact wording found in the MPEP, guiding you directly to the needed information.
- Appendix R, which encompasses all of 37 CFR, is a crucial resource. If you're unsure of an answer or struggling to find information in a specific chapter, starting your search here can be fruitful.
- For questions related to the Patent Cooperation Treaty (PCT), turn to Appendix T (T for Treaty) or Chapter 1800. These sections are dedicated to PCT-related content and can be invaluable for finding answers to PCT-specific questions.

By adopting these strategies, including the judicious use of phrase searches and leveraging the structured organization of the MPEP, you can navigate the exam more effectively and efficiently, enhancing your ability to locate accurate answers and make informed guesses when necessary.

Tackling Practice Exams: Your Path to Success

As crazy as it may sound, practicing with a paper version of the USPTO's previous exams, which are freely available on Wysebridge.com's website here is a great way to mimic exam conditions. Simply print out the pdf of the exam, download the pdf version of the MPEP (available here), and setup shop for 3 or 6 hours depending if you want to do a full or ½ exam. These practice sessions are an invaluable opportunity to familiarize yourself with the exam's format, timing, and content.

Of note, the last official published USPTO Patent Bar Exam was in 2003. Thus, don't expect updated content (and in some instances, don't sweat if you check answers and get a wrong one, or if content doesn't exactly line up.) Take the frustration on the chin so to speak - it's just practice for the sake of familiarity and getting used to searching the MPEP. That is the real benefit here. That being said, we suggest using the 2002/2003 exams to practice with. The prior/older ones really aren't of benefit - however we've included them for archival purposes if you want to explore back.

Creating an Exam-like Environment

For the most beneficial practice experience, simulate the actual exam conditions as closely as possible:

- Isolate Yourself: Choose a quiet, undisturbed location where you can focus without interruptions. This mimics the controlled environment of the exam center.
- Adhere to Time Constraints: Commit to completing each half of the practice exam (three hours each) without breaks, just as in the actual exam setting.
- Prepare Materials: Begin with four sheets of blank paper for your answer grid and several pre-sharpened pencils to avoid any unnecessary interruptions.

Implementing the Answer Grid Strategy

Employ the answer grid method we've discussed previously. This strategy not only helps manage your time effectively but also aids in tracking your confidence level across questions.

MPEP Navigation Practice

When reviewing questions and searching for answers within the MPEP, use Adobe Acrobat or a similar PDF reader for your searches. It's important to note that the search functionalities of Acrobat and Google differ significantly, and you'll only have access to the former during the actual exam. Practicing with the correct tools will equip you with the skills to efficiently find information under exam conditions.

Utilizing Practice Exam Materials

By diligently following these guidelines and incorporating practice exams into your preparation, you'll significantly improve your familiarity with the exam process and increase your chances of success.

Identifying Question Types

The notion of "easy" questions on the Patent Bar Exam is a myth; anticipate every question to challenge your understanding of patent law. A select few questions may seem straightforward, aiming to test your grasp of a single, clear concept. However, the majority will immerse you in complex scenarios, requiring you to sift through extraneous details to identify the critical issue at hand, often involving multiple regulations. You may see some repeated question from prior exams, however, don't count on this as a core tenet of your exam passing strategy.

Strategies for Success

- Understanding Complex Scenarios: Many questions will present a series of events, prompting you to determine the most appropriate response. It's essential to dissect these scenarios, identifying the pivotal actions and regulations involved.
- Timeline Utilization: Crafting a clear timeline can be instrumental in comprehending the sequence of events within a question. Avoid relying on simplistic timeline formats; instead, develop a method that provides clarity and aids in understanding.
- Identifying "Trick" Questions: Essentially, every question could be considered a "trick" question, where minute details hidden within the text hold the key to the correct answer. For instance, recognizing the significance of specific dates or the implications of singular versus plural nouns can be crucial.

Special Considerations

- Foreign Countries and PCT: Pay close attention to the mention of countries, especially in relation to the Patent Cooperation Treaty (PCT), as not all countries are PCT members.
- Time Zones for Submissions: The time zone of submissions (sending versus receiving) can affect the timeliness of your response, depending on the method of submission.
- Names and Terminology: Names may be used to test your attention to detail, and specific terms related to patent applications and actions carry distinct meanings that are critical to understand.

Critical Dates and Document Signatures

- Memorizing Key Dates: Certain dates mark significant changes in law, such as those related to the America Invents Act (AIA). Familiarity with these dates is often directly tested.
- Who Signs What: Understanding which documents require signatures and who is authorized to sign them is another area of focus.

Selecting the "Best" Answer

Often, you'll find that more than one answer could be considered correct. The exam challenges you to select the "best" answer, which may require weighing factors like fees or the best interest of the client. For example, a fee table in Appendix R or a client's specific request in a scenario can guide your decision-making.

Answering Questions Posed in the Negative

Many questions are framed negatively, asking you to identify what is not in accordance with USPTO policy. Recognizing and mentally managing the negatives in these questions is essential for accurate responses.

Efficient Review and Answer Strategy

- Reviewing Your Answers: After selecting an answer, take a moment to mentally justify why it's correct, helping to catch any oversights.
- Comprehensive Question Handling: Address each question fully before moving on to the next, as you may not have time for extensive review later.

Navigating International Patent Applications

International patent applications are filed through the Patent Cooperation Treaty (PCT). While the foundational elements of international patents mirror those of U.S. patents—comprising a title, abstract, specification, claims, and drawings, alongside rights for priority claims, restrictions against new matter in amendments, and entitlement to an interview—the process diverges significantly in flow, terminology, and procedural specifics when compared to the U.S. system. For instance, the term "a single inventive concept" in U.S. patent parlance is referred to as "unity of invention" under the PCT. This difference in terminology underscores the broader variations between the two systems.

To navigate these differences effectively, we advise studying the PCT rules, detailed in MPEP chapter 1800, distinctly from the rest of the MPEP, which focuses on U.S. procedures. This approach helps prevent confusion between the two systems.

Creating a comprehensive timeline at the outset of your PCT studies is a beneficial strategy. Regularly updating and referring to this timeline can enhance your understanding of the PCT process. Consider including key milestones such as:
- The date of any prior-filed application for priority claims
- The filing date of the current application
- Actions taken by the Receiving Office (RO) and International Bureau (IB)
- The initiation and completion of the International Search Report (ISR)
- Deadlines for amendments
- The timing for submitting the Demand
- Actions by the International Preliminary Examination Authority (IPEA)
- Due dates for fees
- Publication dates or when the application is made available to the public
- Deadlines for entering the National Stage and associated actions
- Priority claim deadlines
-

By meticulously plotting these points on your timeline, you can gain a clearer picture of the PCT process, making it easier to distinguish from the U.S. patent system and improving your mastery of international patenting procedures.

Essentials to Know for the Patent Bar Exam

Upon first delving into the myriad of procedural rules concerning signatures, communication with the office, and various deadlines, the amount of information might seem daunting to memorize. Yet, you'll find that these procedures and deadlines are predominantly logical and consistent.

For instance, the guidelines on what cannot be faxed are extensive yet intuitive. Color documents and those necessitating an original signature are understandably ineligible for faxing. Similarly, it's logical that documents subject to secrecy orders, original applications, disciplinary hearings, and contested cases before the Patent Trial and Appeal Board (PTAB) cannot be faxed.

When it comes to deadlines, there's a general consistency to grasp. Many exam questions revolve around deadlines, so committing these to memory will serve you well. Statutory deadlines are typically non-negotiable, barring exceptional circumstances with sufficient justification; conversely, nonstatutory deadlines can often be extended through surcharges. Certain statutory deadlines, especially those related to appeals and issuance, are set at two months. Except for the application fee, all fees are due upon service request. The PCT system allows for slightly more leniency in fee deadlines.

The standard timeframe to respond to an office action is three months, with an absolute six-month statutory limit, beyond which no extensions are granted. Error corrections usually grant a one-month window, while certain notifications, like amendments to non-publication requests, might have a specific day requirement, such as 45 days.

Extensions can be categorized into two types: for cause and for fee. The latter merely requires a fee payment and a request for an extension, which is then automatically granted. The former, however, necessitates a petition accompanied by a fee, a valid reason matching the allowable causes, substantial evidence, and is subject to office approval.

Missing a statutory deadline can lead to patent abandonment, a situation that, while reversible, demands proof that the delay was "unavoidable" to successfully revive the application.
All these guidelines, however, shift when it comes to the PCT. It's crucial to study PCT-specific deadlines and procedures independently to avoid confusion, given their unique requirements and timeframes.

We provide a host of must know facts and quick memorization tips to focus on at wysebridge.com.

Exam Day Success: Tips and Strategies

Plan to arrive early at the testing center, as the check-in process may be unexpectedly slow, and there's likely to be a crowd. Don't forget, it's a general testing center (not just specific for the USPTO Patent Bar Exam).

It's best to leave your cell phone, electronics, and study materials in your car. Any items you bring will be stored in a locker, and access to these lockers may be restricted until the test concludes.

For simplicity and to avoid unnecessary hassle, leave accessories like watches, sweaters, scarves, jackets, caps, hats, and even capes in your car, especially if the weather permits. You'll be required to remove these items before entering the test room and demonstrate empty, inverted pockets.

Essentially, the only items you should bring into the test center are your car keys, the test acknowledgment letter, and valid identification. Ensure you have at least two forms of ID, with one being a government-issued photo ID, and verify that the name on your test acknowledgment letter exactly matches that on your ID.
If you need to take medication, be aware that its administration will be monitored and stored in your locker, necessitating check-outs and check-ins from the test room, consuming precious time.

Consider moderating your caffeine intake to minimize bathroom breaks, which also eat into your exam time.

Be prepared for the testing center's security measures, including being photographed and fingerprinted, potentially more than once.

Don't forget to pause and take a breath now and then during the exam. Give yourself the space to be, and then focus back in.

Next Steps After Passing: Launching Your Patent Career

Immediately after completing the exam, you will learn whether you have passed. In the past, candidates may have received a notification of failure, only to be informed of a passing result later on. This discrepancy occurred as the USPTO occasionally made "post-test" adjustments for questions that were not scored or removed from the scoring process due to recent legal developments or policy changes. However, this is no longer the case (and in fact, an appeal process is no longer available to test takers).

Upon successfully passing the exam, the USPTO will send you a letter offering you the opportunity to register as a patent practitioner, which includes a fee (of course). There's a review period to assess your "good moral character," followed by an additional 15 to 25 days for processing. You can anticipate checking your status online a week or two before receiving official confirmation through mail.

Now begins the real journey of mastering patent drafting and prosecution. There are numerous resources at your disposal, ranging from free materials to more expensive courses and guides, all designed to aid in your professional development as a patent practitioner. If you need some suggestions or support, feel free to contact us anytime!

Conclusion

As you reach the end of this guide, we at Wysebridge.com want to congratulate you on the dedication and hard work you've put into preparing for the Patent Bar Exam. The journey to becoming a patent practitioner is rigorous and challenging, but immensely rewarding. The strategies, insights, and tips provided here are designed to equip you with the knowledge and skills necessary to navigate the exam confidently and successfully. Remember, the path to mastering patent law and prosecution is a continuous learning process, extending far beyond passing the exam.

Embrace each step of this journey with the same commitment and enthusiasm you've shown so far. We wish you all the best as you move forward.

May your efforts lead to success on the exam and in your future career in patent law. Good luck, and may your career as a patent practitioner be fulfilling and prosperous.

With warmest regards,

The Wysebridge Team

wysebridge.com